Advance Praise for

THRIVING

"*Thriving* is a brilliant and comprehensive overview of the burgeoning movement to regenerate our land, products, forests, cities, and society. Wayne's infectious optimism is borne from the possibilities that are emerging when people fully embrace the ecological and social crises we face and human imagination aligns with the life of the planet."

—Paul Hawken, author of *Regeneration: Ending the Climate Crisis in One Generation*

"A key insight of the theory of living systems is the realization that life, at all levels, is inherently regenerative. In this book the author explores the social, economic, and political implications of this insight, which are critical to overcoming our multifaceted crisis. He skillfully lays out a coherent framework for regeneration, illustrated with countless examples of innovative solutions, at the levels of ecosystems, societies, economies, and organizations. An inspiring and tremendously hopeful book!"

—Fritjof Capra, author of *The Hidden Connections* and *The Systems View of Life*

"Visser's book is not just another call to action—it is a must-read guide for how businesses can realise their potential by fundamentally changing their relationship with nature, society, and the economy."

—Mads Nipper, CEO of Ørsted